Intuition
Pathway to Destiny

James Culver Bryant

∞INFINITY
PUBLISHING

Intuition
Pathway to Destiny

by

James Culver Bryant

TO: Veronica & Denise
I enjoyed meeting you both.

Keep being amazing and
unstoppable!

Jim Bryant

7/17

Copyright © 2015 by James Culver Bryant

ISBN 978-1-4958-0592-9
ISBN 978-1-4958-0593-6 eBook

Published May 2015

INFINITY PUBLISHING
1094 New DeHaven Street, Suite 100
West Conshohocken, PA 19428-2713
Toll-free (877) BUY BOOK
Local Phone (610) 941-9999
Fax (610) 941-9959
Info@buybooksontheweb.com
www.buybooksontheweb.com

Also by James Culver Bryant

Coming Together: Healing Body, Mind and Spirit

CONTENTS

INTRODUCTION

There is purpose to every life. What if you had a pathway to fulfill your destiny—your life's purpose? Wouldn't you be interested in learning about that path in order succeed in achieving your destiny? I had these questions in mind when I wrote this book. I did not have a book to read when I was growing up in the 1940s and 50s to help me find the answer to what life was all about. I decided to write this book, so that others might find some answers and learn from my experiences, as well as from those who contributed to this book by telling their stories.

Finding your purpose is possible by learning to listen and by being in touch with your intuition. How to follow your intuition is addressed in the chapter about how to get out of your own way. Sometimes we intuitively know what to do, but can't act for one reason or another. Usually fear gets in our way.

A central theme of this book is to surrender to the journey of life. Life cannot be figured out by thinking your way through each step. Instead, participating in the process of life without knowing how events will turn out is key to experiencing your destiny. When I decided to join the military in order to become a pilot, I had no idea that I would be turned down by the Air Force and the Army, because I only had an Associate's Degree. How could I have known that a Navy recruiter would overhear my conversation with the Air Force recruiter and invite me to try out for the Navy's Naval Aviation Cadet program? I went along with the journey that presented itself with the Navy, instead of what I originally wanted, which was a career in the Air Force. I have never regretted my decision.

I invite you to learn from ordinary people who found themselves in extraordinary situations. Their accounts of how they managed to cope with unique circumstances illustrate the role of intuition and meaningful coincidences (synchronicity). In addition, there are stories of how people found themselves in careers that they would never have imagined, and a destiny none could foretell.

I searched for the secret of life, until I found mine. No one could ever have told me, because if they had, I would not have believed them. I had to experience life, before the secret presented itself. For me, the secret is to live each day by showing up and doing my best. Only I can know what *showing up* and *doing my best* means for me, because that is how I have tried to live. Your secret of life is out there for you to discover. The chapters that follow provide a map that can guide you to experience your destiny and discover your personal secret of life.

Chapter One

Surrendering to Intuition

My life continues to show me that following my intuition works best. Not surprisingly, my Myers Briggs Personality Test indicates that I have strong intuitive characteristics. Looking back at the professions and the hobbies I have chosen, I see a pattern of choices where thinking my way through a situation would not have worked. There just wasn't enough time to think.

I followed my intuition to join the Navy in early 1961 instead of waiting to be drafted. The idea of slogging through a Vietnamese jungle wet and miserable was a situation that I hoped to avoid. Flying, on the other hand, was something I really wanted to do, so I thought I'd fulfill my military obligation while having the Navy provide the flying lessons. At 21, I really didn't know what I was doing, or what I was getting into. I sold my Corvette, because the monthly payments were more than my monthly Navy pay, and found myself in the

Indoctrination Battalion in Pensacola, Florida wondering what I had done.

This snippet of my life's story contains everything I needed to know about life, but I couldn't see it at the time. In retrospect, I can see that I really didn't have a plan other than doing what attracted my attention, like wanting to be a pilot. There was no master plan. In fact, as I look back, I was coping one day at a time, living in fear of failure, which would have resulted in my being washed-out of the flight program and sent to the fleet as a sailor.

Looking back on the situation, I noticed that I left my home in Redwood City, CA and moved to Pensacola, FL, because my life in Redwood City was over. My childhood was over, and my future was going to be found elsewhere.

Learning to fly is another example of following my intuition. I already knew how to fly, because I paid for flight lessons and had around ten hours of flight time, before I joined the Navy. The first thing my flight instructor told me was to forget everything that I thought I knew about flying. I was going to learn how the Navy wanted me to fly. In order to become a carrier pilot, I had to follow the rules and perform up to the Navy's expectations, or be washed out of flight training. I also had to pay attention to my intuition that saved my life on more occasions than I can remember. I was young and inexperienced, so intuition was all I really had going for me. I was also invincible–a necessary condition for a young aviator.

Being a young aviator was great fun, because I was unencumbered by experience. I didn't know what I couldn't do, so I didn't hold back. It's a wonder that I survived. As time went on and I became more senior, I would tell my junior officers that I wanted their thoughts, because I needed their fresh eyes and ideas. I knew what I knew, and that was limiting. What a concept. The only way that I could increase my knowledge was to recognize that I did not know everything and to listen for new ideas. I noticed that a few of the senior officers around me had stopped listening and believed that they knew everything. They just wanted subordinates to carry out orders. I knew that I couldn't operate that way. I liked to "wing it" (no aviation pun intended) more than just follow orders.

"Winging it" required that I get out of my own way, listen more, and know less. I had learned that listening, or being aware of what I noticed, was very important. When I retired, I started to make a life-changing transition. This was another major event where my intuition was apparent. I heard a public service announcement on the radio asking for hospice volunteers. I don't know why I noticed the announcement, but I followed through and asked if I could help out. My role was to sit with patients who were in a coma and talk with their family members, who were about to lose their loved one. I would also help the nurses care for those who were in the process of dying. One day the social worker on staff asked me if I had ever considered becoming a social worker. I laughed, because the thought of going from naval aviator to social worker had never entered my mind. I then remembered someone, who was a former Viet Nam carrier pilot, who had done that very thing and the rest, as they say, is history. I had begun my transition from naval officer to social worker, and what could be more intuitive than that.

I received my Masters Degree in Social Work from The Catholic University of America, which introduced me to the various psychodynamic practice theories. My education was great, because it gave me a toolbox full of tools that I could use to help others. I still had to learn how to use the tools, and this would require that I combine the science that I learned in graduate school with the art of applying my intuition. As I gained experience, I discovered that traditional psychotherapy practice methods did not work for some clients. Their wounds went untouched by established approaches. So again I followed my intuition, and I began to change the way that I worked with my clients.

I had the opportunity to develop my treatment approach and my skills, because of a woman I met while I was working in the Arlington County Detention Facility (jail) as a mental health therapist. (Let's call her Jane.) Jane was arrested for shoplifting, but she couldn't remember doing the deed. I learned that she had no memory of taking anything and was shocked when the police found costume jewelry in her purse.

Normally, I wouldn't have believed her story. Inmates tend to deny the charges against them. However, this inmate was well dressed, in her forties, a professional, and could have bought anything that she wanted. Most noticeable, too, was the fact that items taken from her purse didn't fit her personality, because they were all something a young teen would want.

I saw Jane several times a week while she was in jail and tried to figure out why, about every six months, she would end up in jail with a shoplifting charge. I discovered that she had a part of her personality that had split off during an extremely dangerous time of her life, when she was a teenager. She would have to steal food for her family in a country that would have locked her up for a long time, if she was caught. The stress of having to do what her family needed was too traumatic, causing her as a young teen to dissociate.[1]

As life went on, stressful situations would trigger the dissociated teen part to take over and do what she knew best–steal. In addition to having a dissociative disorder, Jane suffered from various pains that the doctors could never diagnose. It was clear that Jane's issues were very complex, and I didn't think traditional talk therapy was going to solve all of her problems.

Jane contacted me six months after being released from jail and asked if she could see me in my private practice. This situation created the opportunity for me to begin to explore the effectiveness of alternative solutions to both her dissociative disorder and her mysterious pains. She agreed to a treatment plan that included energy work in combination with hypnosis.

---

[1] **Dissociation:** In psychology and psychiatry, a perceived detachment of the mind from the emotional state or even from the body.

I learned how to do energy work, when I took a workshop based on the book, *Hands of Light: A Guide to Healing Through the Human Energy Field* by Barbara Brennan and Jos. A. Smith. I discovered during the workshop that the techniques worked for me, because when I used them, I was able to release some of my old anger. I was then able to help others in the workshop find relief from old traumas. As for the hypnosis treatment, I became certified as an Advanced Hypnotherapist by the National Guild of Hypnotists. During that certification process, I experienced the effectiveness of hypnosis on myself and others. The idea of combining hypnosis and energy work must have come from my intuition, because I had never heard of it before.

Jane's pain turned out to be psychosomatic pain[2] associated with stress. Jane held her stress in her neck and shoulders. Being hypnotized during the energy work meant that Jane's mind was deeply relaxed. With her mind relaxed and essentially out of her way, I was able to work with the pain and find ways for Jane to release her stress without storing it in her body. As for Jane's teenage disso-ciated part, I used hypnosis to treat the teen's traumatic memories and then blend the teen part back into Jane's personality system.

The treatment worked. Ten years after her treatment ended, Jane contacted me to say that she had no more unexplainable pains and no more problems with the law. In retrospect, the timing was perfect. Jane came into

---

[2] Psychosomatic pain is a pain disorder associated with psychological factors.

my life just as I was ready to expand my approach to therapy. Meeting Jane worked for both of us. This is a good example of synchronicity.

The next experience that expanded my belief system as to what was normal came with a client who called for an immediate appointment. (Let's call her Mary.) Mary reported having a panic attack while shopping at Home Depot. She had never had a panic attack before and was afraid of having another. During our discussion of what was going on just before she felt the panic coming on, Mary said she heard the clacking sound of a wheel on one of the store's shopping carts. I suggested that we use hypnosis to follow the clacking sound and see where the sound took us.

Well, what happened next was very unexpected. Mary saw herself in a horse-drawn cart with several other women. The cart was being pulled over cobblestones, making the same sound that she heard before her panic attack. I asked where the cart was taking her, and she said it was taking her to be burned at the stake. Next, she was telling me that she was smelling smoke and getting very hot. I accelerated the scene to after she died and brought her back to normal consciousness. Mary had no problem understanding why she was burned at the stake. She said she had always had a problem being blunt and speaking "out of turn." She figured that she was burned at the stake, because she rebelled at the rules of her people–something she said that she continues to do.

Up until this experience, I didn't know if I believed in past lives. The teachings of my Christian upbringing didn't support the belief in past lives. Yet, Eastern religions did. I decided to take the experience at face value. Who am I to judge?

As I look back on situations that created turning points in my life, I am able to recognize how I was guided. Now, in retrospect, I recognize everything that happened was getting me ready for whatever was coming next. I learned that as long as I allowed my clients to tell their stories and not judge and disregard what they were experiencing, they would lead me to exactly where they needed to go. I also learned to follow my intuition and not to restrict myself.

Listening and allowing my clients to take me beyond the limits of traditional methodology created the space for me to evolve both as a clinician and as a person. A teacher taught me to hold loosely what I thought I knew. In this way, any new understandings could replace my obsolete ideas. What I had understood to be normal needed to be flexible enough to change. I was living in a structure that wasn't big enough. It was like my house had to expand to hold new ideas and new ways to think and live.

My traditional framework of what was possible or impossible was very limiting. My childhood experience, along with that of being in the military, provided a relatively limited view of life. The old framework was developed around following the rules and agreeing with the beliefs of others, which limited my psychological freedom. As I freed myself from the limitations formed by my past, I found myself working to help others become psychologically free, so they could exercise free will and free choice. A new framework was needed that would not restrict the possible. The new framework was necessary to allow me the flexibility to fulfill my purpose.

I believe the most important thing that I did during my transition to this new framework was to surrender what I thought I knew, and who I thought I was, and to allow a new identity to form. This new framework required me to *not know* and to be able to listen and allow words to flow through me and not own them. I discovered that my rational mind was very limited, because its operating system was based on having to know the answer, which had always been what I expected from myself. When I stopped attempting to meet what I thought were the expectations of others and myself, I was able to stop thinking so much and receive exactly what I needed in the moment.

Sometimes we find ourselves in a situation where we have no choice other than operating moment by moment and allowing our intuition to take charge. I learned this by watching my wife, Meg Falk, during the events of September 11, 2001. I learned that a crisis pulls us out of our comfort zone and drops us in the deep end of the pool where we sink or swim. There is no time to pick up a manual or hire an expert. There is no time, because there is only now, the moment we are in. Listening to our intuitive guidance becomes our best resource. When we get beyond the crisis, we are able to look back and see how, when we followed our intuition, we made all the right decisions.

Chapter Two

Intuition
and Synchronicity

⌐⟶⌐

I asked my wife, Meg Falk, to tell her story of what happened on September 11, 2001, because it is a great example of intuition and synchronicity at work.

Meg Falk's Story

I was holding a staff meeting in the Pentagon on 9/11. At 9:37 a.m., there was a huge thud, and the building shook. What followed was the culmination of what I had learned through the years, and the wisdom that I had received from the people who I had met along the way.

As the Director of the Office of Family Policy for the Secretary of Defense, I had policy responsibility for Military Family Support, Casualty Assistance and Mortuary Affairs. Little did I know that these seemingly divergent responsibilities would come into critical play in the days ahead. We thought the thud and building shaking were maintenance-related and continued our meeting until told to evacuate. At this point, we knew nothing about the World Trade Center. I told my staff to call their loved ones and let them know we were all right. I called my husband, Jim, at work and left a message that said, "No matter what you see or what you hear, I am all right." We then proceeded to evacuate.

During my years at the Pentagon, whenever I was outside and saw a plane flying over the Pentagon going from or to National Airport, I thought to myself, if a plane ever hits the Pentagon, the first thing I am going to do is contact Jim and let him know that I am all right. I had learned this from my dear friend, Sharon Bryson, who at the time headed the Family Assistance Office at the National Transportation Safety Board (NTSB). In the course of one of our dinners together, she told me that all airlines require their employees, whether they are ticket takers or baggage handlers, to call home immediately, if there ever is a plane mishap. This was to prevent airline family members from clogging up the toll free number that airlines are required to set up after any plane crash. The memory of this conversation came back to me on 9/11. As it turned out for my staff and me, letting our loved ones know that we were all right before we left the building prevented a lot of grief and worry for family and friends.

We knew that we had casualties given the horrible black smoke rising from the next wedge of the Pentagon. With a few of my staff still with me, we drove a short distance to an Air Force office where we started locating key Pentagon staff. Coming out of my daze that followed the attack, I suddenly realized: "We need to set up a Family Assistance Center for the families of the missing." This is a tradition in the Department of Defense (DoD) whenever there is a multiple casualty incident. The lessons I learned from previous mass casualty incidents would prove to be invaluable for the events that followed.

I obtained permission from the Under Secretary of Defense for Personnel and Readiness to set up the Family Assistance Center. He directed me to have it functioning by the next day, so that it could be announced at the Pentagon briefing the following morning. We were "in the zone," making decisions left and right. To this day, we are still amazed that just four of us were able to make it all happen.

Over the years, my friend Sharon Bryson, who I mentioned earlier, shared a number of important best practices that the NTSB used following an airline mishap. Among others, these included taking over a hotel, keeping media from intruding on the families, holding two briefings a day, and allowing families to go to the site where their loved one perished. All of these shared practices came to mind during decision making on 9/11.

An important tactical decision was to avoid establishing the Center on a military installation. I intuitively knew that if we set up the Center on a military base, security would be too tight, and many of the affected families would not be able to access the Center, if they lacked proper ID. My staff was able to locate a hotel. The hotel manager took us in on a handshake.

He didn't even know if he would get paid. Eventually, he did. We then proceeded to call other Departmental and non-Departmental organizations for assistance. This assistance included mental health staff, chaplains, child care, medical, civilian personnel, the Services Casualty Assistance offices, legal, the FBI, the NTSB, the Dover Mortuary, and Security to keep the press away from the families who wanted their privacy.

All of the organizations that we asked on 9/11 to come to the Center were vital to the support of the families of the missing. To this day, I look back and am astonished that the decisions that we made on 9/11 would turn out to be exactly what was needed. On that awful day, I was also inspired to call the Norfolk Family Service Center for assistance as they, unfortunately, had gone through the experience of setting up a Family Assistance Center the prior year in the aftermath of the USS Cole bombing, Fortunately, the Director of the Center was my good friend and colleague, Cathy Stokoe. She and six staff drove up that night to assist. They were critical in our ability to set up the Center overnight.

The next morning at 7:00 a.m., there were 40 volunteers from the Pentagon setting up and staffing the Center. I announced the opening of the Pentagon Family Assistance Center (PFAC) at the Pentagon briefing on September 12, and the families of the missing started to come. With the wide range of organizational support right there at the PFAC, the grieving families did not have to go around to all these organizations for assistance. The support services were all in one place for them, making the agony of their loss less burdensome.

As word of the PFAC spread, even more family members started to show up. Also, the Casualty Assistance Officers assigned to the military and civilian families and the families of those on Flight #77 arrived to help. We briefed the families twice a day. Sometimes there would be hundreds of people in the ballroom during the briefings. It was the one place families could go where they knew they would get accurate information, as there were many false rumors during those dark days. Other organizations (e.g., Therapy Dogs, Red Cross) also started arriving to assist, and we had virtually every possible type of support available for the families on site. As my husband often reminds me, "You had a great idea, and it is a good thing so many showed up to save your butt." Very true.

The PFAC was a supportive, safe haven for those experiencing the worse loss of their lives. As one young son said to the Child Care staff, "I like being here. You understand what I am going through." We operated the PFAC 24/7 for a month. My experience at the Center was the most intense time of my life.

As I look back, I see that so many experiences, colleagues, and friends had prepared me for that tragic day in American history The lessons I culled from previous DoD mass casualty incidents helped form in my mind what we needed to do immediately. The best practices and lessons learned from my colleagues at the NTSB, the FBI, and the Military Service Family Centers profoundly influenced the decisions made and actions taken in establishing and running the PFAC. My direct interaction with the families from the 1996 CT-43 plane crash in Croatia that killed the Commerce Secretary Ron Brown and 34 others taught me to always keep the families first – the guiding principle of the PFAC. The CT-43 families also taught me that each person handles grief and loss in their own way. No two people grieve the same. It was during the meetings with the CT-43 families that I met my good friend, Kathryn Turman, Director of Victim Assistance for the FBI. Through the years, Kathryn has shared with me many lessons learned on how best to assist victims of violence and terrorism. I watched how she interacted with the families of the victims from Black Hawk Down in Somalia, Pan Am 103, and Khobar Towers, to name a few. She is always the compassionate professional keeping the families first, and she is exquisitely sensitive to the many needs of victims' families. All of these influences and experiences came to bear on that fateful day and for the duration of the PFAC.

I am grateful to all those who have "gifted" me along the way with their wisdom and willingness to pass on their lessons learned. What they shared with me played an essential role in my ability to be "in the zone" and listen to my intuition following the 9/11 Pentagon attack.

****

Meg's account of her taking charge and developing a plan to address the tragedy that happened on 9/11 illustrates that she was well prepared to go into action.

Previous experiences, along with information she had gained from her good friends at the FBI and the NTSB, all came into play. I wondered if Meg had other experiences where following her intuition had a profound impact upon herself or others. Here is what she said.

One of my Casualty policy responsibilities as Director of Family Policy was military funeral honors. In the late 1990s, as many as 12,000 World War II veterans were dying each day. This was at the same time that the military force was downsizing. As a result, when family members wanted funeral honors for their veteran, the Military Services often were unable to provide them due to lack of personnel. The Veterans Service Organizations (VSOs) were very displeased with the Department of Defense for not providing this service. So, we decided that instead of going head-to-head with the VSOs, we would invite them to collaborate with us on a solution. After many meetings and focus groups on the issue, we agreed that the most important elements of funeral honors were: the folding and presentation of the flag and the sounding of Taps. We likewise agreed that at least one member of the military funeral group should be from the branch of service in which the veteran served. In addition, we received authority for the Reserves to help with this effort. All requests would be honored and handled by the Services through a toll free number, when requested by the family through their funeral director. Seemingly, the problem was solved.

My gut was telling me that the problem was not solved, and that the dignified delivery of funeral honors was marred by the fact that real buglers were not available for most veterans funerals and Taps was played by a boom box. The tapes used were often scratched and lacked quality sound. My intuition told me there had to be a better way.

I thought that with modern technology, we could come up with some sort of digital bugle that would sound Taps even though the person holding it did not know how to play a bugle. This would significantly elevate the dignity of the funeral honors ceremony. When I floated this idea up the chain, I was told it was a crazy idea, probably not possible, that it wasn't worth the effort, and that veterans' families would feel deceived. My instinct told me otherwise, so I went under the radar to pursue this "crazy" concept.

Working with our contractor, Tony Minor, I asked him to get in touch with major sound companies to see if they were interested in developing something like this. None of them were. I asked Tony to keep on trying. Coincidentally, he was meeting with a friend of his in New York and told him what I wanted developed. His friend, Simon Britt from the UK, turned out to be a sound engineer who said, "Let me take a look at it." Fast forward. Simon developed a prototype bugle that played taps digitally, and some months later we demonstrated it at the Pentagon. Several of my superiors were still a bit dubious about the veterans' families and VSOs accepting it. Nonetheless, they asked Simon to go back and make a few improvements. I deliberately kept all of these plans quiet as my gut was telling me that once the word of the bugle got out, everyone would want one immediately. I was right.

We held a big meeting with all the VSOs and part of that meeting included the premiering of the "Ceremonial Bugle." We first brought in the premier bugler from Arlington National Cemetery who played Taps on a real bugle. Then we brought out the "Ceremonial Bugle" and it, too, sounded Taps perfectly. The crowd went wild. As I expected, they all wanted one right away.

The innovation of the "Ceremonial Bugle" was featured on local news and national media. When people in England found out about it, they contacted Simon and asked him "What are you going to do for the homeland?" As a result, all countries in the Commonwealth now have "Ceremonial Bugles" that sound Last Post, which is their Taps.

The most rewarding thing about all of this is that now thousands of veterans' funeral honors ceremonies all over the world are more dignified and give greater respect to those who served their nations.

Following one's instinct, in spite of doubts all around, can result in large rewards for many. In this case, it is our veterans who are so deserving of dignity and respect at their funerals.

****

I love this story because it begins with an intuitive belief that something could be done to fix a problem. Then it describes how circumstances unfolded to bring the Ceremonial Bugle into reality. Meg's story also demonstrates how she did not let others stop her from doing what she believed was the right thing to do. This theme is echoed in the stories that follow.

Meg, Kathryn Turman, and Sharon Bryson continue to get together over dinner to catch up and just enjoy visiting with each other. On one such occasion, each agreed to share their stories of how intuition and synchronicity have influenced their lives.

Kathryn Turman's Story

When I was a kid, I went to summer camp and everybody at camp and in my junior high had a crush on this older boy named Jeff. When I was in college at the University of Texas, he was a graduate student in architecture, and I ran into him on campus one day. Well lo and behold, he asked me to go out. We had this wonderful kind of romance and developed a relationship and then got engaged. About two months after we got engaged, he was diagnosed with a brain tumor, and I spent the next year and a half going through that with him. He passed away. So when my fellow students were going to graduation, I went to his funeral. That was tough.

I graduated and moved to Dallas with my roommate. We started doing things, and then I started to approach the age of 25, and all of my friends were getting married. I hadn't thought much about what I was going to be doing in the future. I thought I was going to be married and go on, but that didn't work out. So my friends were getting married, and I started dating this guy who was very nice.

He was my best friend's fiancé's law school partner. So we had a lot of fun, a nice guy, and we got engaged.

I got all the way to three weeks before the wedding, when I heard something in my mind saying that this wasn't right–but I was on this sort of train. Then my fiancé's younger brother Robin was in town, and we had lunch together. He looked at me and asked if I was really sure I wanted to do this. "So what do you mean?" I asked. He said, "I know my brother, and I've gotten to know you, and I just don't see this, particularly for you, being a good thing." He said, "You know him, and you know my mother." I thought about it and decided he was right. I decided to call it off three weeks before the wedding. I called my maid of honor and my best friends and my dad, and they all said, "Thank God. We don't have anything against him. He's not a bad guy, but forget it. He's just not the right person for you."

They were right, so I called it off. My dad said, "I'll tell your mother. Take your bridesmaids and your friends and go to Mexico for a week." We did, and he was right. I was rebounding to some degree and just reacting to what I thought I should be doing. Calling it off made me stop and think. "What do I want from my life?" I spent a lot of time thinking on that beach in Mexico with a couple of margaritas a day. "What is it that I want?"

A few years ago, I saw one of my college roommates who was going to be my maid of honor, and we had a good laugh. She said, "You remember the night before we graduated, we were at my parents lake house." We were talking about our plans that night, and she knew she was gong to be a teacher, and I wasn't sure what I wanted to do. She reminded me, "You told me that night that you weren't sure where you were going, but you were sure you wanted your life to be more than something long." She commented, "If you had married what's his name, you would be…" I said, "I know what I would be. I would be an alcoholic, country club housewife, in Houston, chasing the pool boy around the cabana." That decision to call off my wedding taught me to listen to my instincts. It taught me to listen to my gut.

Author: How do you listen to your gut–your instincts?

Kathryn Turman: The first time with Robin telling me it was crazy to marry his brother, I was acknowledging, "Yes, you're right." It helps to have somebody else reflect it, and ask me the right question. "Is this what you really want to do?" He validated my inner doubt, my gut feeling. He had gotten me to think it through, for which I am forever grateful. After that, I just learned to stop, and every year or so I would just sit down and think, "Am I on the track I want to go on?" The thing I learned a long time ago is that you can lay all the great plans you want–and people should have goals and think about what you want to do, and think about who you are and what you want to become–but at the end of the day, life can upset those plans, and you may diverge for awhile. Ultimately, I really think that if you listen to it (intuition), the deep desires of our heart will find its way, if you let it.

Author: How did you learn to "let it?"

Kathryn Turman: I think that experience helped me a lot. I just started thinking, "What is it I really want out of life?" For me it was, "I want my life to have some meaning. I want to do something that is bigger than myself." That was always important to me, since I was a little kid. I think that even though it meant that I would not have everything.

My grandfather used to tell me, "If you can have everything in your life, where would you put it?" It was a kind of a tongue-in-cheek way of saying, you can't have everything in your life. So if you choose this, you may not end up choosing this other. Be content with where you go and with your choices along the way, and don't blame other people for your choices, if they don't work out very well.

On my 25th birthday I sat down and said, "Okay, in five years I'm going to be 30, and where do I want to be? I want to own my home. I want to be in a good relationship. I want to travel, and I want to have my good friends around me." At age 30, I owned my own home. I was in what turned out to be an eleven-year loving relationship. We were traveling, and I had a lot of friends. We went sailing every summer. We had a great time.

Author: The message I heard was that you learned to trust your gut.

Kathryn Turman: Yes, and also to recognize, too, that I had to figure out what I want. I remember when one of my best friends turned 40. We were going to get ice-cream, and all of a sudden she exclaimed, "I'm 40, and I'm never going to be a nuclear physicist." I said, "What! Have you ever wanted to be a nuclear physicist?" She responded with, "Well, no." I then said to her, "You were in drama and a fund raiser, and you have four kids at home. Why do you want to be a nuclear physicist?" "It would give me more options." I said, "That's ridiculous. Things happen all the time, and people just have to reinvent their lives. If you want to do something, then plan for it. Your kids are going to grow eventually." You know what she is doing now? She is out in California and has a movie production company. Not a nuclear physicist. She went back to her drama background.

****

Kathryn's position with the FBI, mentioned in Meg's story about 9/11, has allowed her to have a major impact on the lives of so many people. Her story shows how events throughout her life guided her to fulfill her fundamental goal of making a difference. As she has said, "I want my life to have some meaning. I want to do something that is bigger than myself. That was always important to me, since I was a little kid."

This was her guiding principle, and her intuition supported it. She knew who she was and what she wanted as a kid. Kathryn developed the practice of trusting her intuition and created the space necessary to receive its guidance. She also listened to others who, at a critical time, validated her instincts not to marry someone whom she thought that she should marry.

****

Author: Sharon, would you tell us a story of when your intuition helped you through a situation?

Sharon Bryson's Story

There are just so many of them, when you're doing Family Center work. I guess there are certain rules of engagement, when you're building a family assistance response. There are so many things you can't predict. During the response to the Buffalo accident,[3] we were doing a site visit for all the family members. (It is important to many victims' family members to go to the exact place where their loved one perished.) However, in Buffalo there was a really bad snowstorm coming in. We knew if we were going to do a site visit, we had to do it quickly, and at the same time, we were having difficulty recovering all the remains. Some of the remains were in the basement of one of the houses that was hit by the airplane.

The rule is that you never do a site visit, of course, with remains still on the scene. If we waited, there would be such a horrific snowstorm that everything would be covered. So you're in that mode of what are you going to do? I remember the team standing there looking at me wanting an answer. "What are we going to do, Sharon, and which way are you going to call it?" I remember having the thought that we really have to take this to the people to whom this is most important–the families. I said to the team, "We're going to have to go into the family briefing

---

[3] Colgan Air Flight 2407 crashed near Buffalo, N.Y. on February 12, 2009.

as a team and explain to them, here is what we would like to do for you. If we do the site visit, you need to understand that the recovery is not over. There are still remains being recovered. We would never, ever consider taking families, except we have extraordinary weather circumstances. We need your help in deciding whether that's the right thing to do or not. My sense is that it is the right thing to do."

So we showed them what it would look like. We gave them the visual, the direction from which we would approach and told them they would not see the remains, because they are in the basement of the house. I said to them, "I want you to understand. I don't want you to find out afterwards. I don't want you to hear it from anybody but me, that we made an intentional decision to take you out there for the site visit."

So we just laid it out there for them. One of the gentlemen in the room who was pretty outspoken, I'll never forget, raised his hand, and I thought, well here it goes. Here goes the house of cards. He said, "I just have one question. Will taking us out there for the site visit delay the return of anyone's loved ones remains?" Of course, that's a question asked without any understanding of process. Because no matter how long it takes us to do the on-scene recovery, there is still a whole other process over here that is going to take days and weeks. They were not at that point of understanding yet. I said to him, "No it won't. It will not make a bit of difference. It is still going to take weeks to get to that point. The difference is that if we don't do the site visit today, you'll lose that opportunity, because of the weather that's moving in. As a family group, you have to decide if that's the right thing to do. I'm willing to do it. I want everybody here to be comfortable with it, so take a few minutes. I'll be back."

We walked out into the hallway and the team said to me, "That's pretty risky for you to go in there and ask them to make that decision." It just seemed to be the right thing to do. I just couldn't make that decision for them, because there were just too many variables.

So, they collectively made a decision that they were all comfortable with. We did the site visit and paused the recovery process. They came back, and what was very interesting to me was to see the difference in their affect. When they returned from the site visit, they were in a whole different place than they were beforehand.

I can tell when the intuition has kicked in, because the other team members will have a reaction to me. They will say something like, "Whoa, wait a minute. Where is that in the plan book?" It isn't in the plan book. That's just a fact. Those are just some of the things you end up having to go with in situations like this one.

Elaine, who I worked with for a long time, repeatedly said to me, "Always trust your gut. It's the best place to make decisions. Those are the best decisions you've made. When you shut that down, and don't listen to it any more, that's when you run into problems. You really have to trust those gut instincts."

Kathryn Turman: I remember when we played the voice recorder of Flight 93[4] for the 9/11 families, Sharon and I talked a lot about that at the time. Bob Mueller, the Acting Director of the FBI, called me and said, "Everyone is calling me and telling me not to play this—lawyers, all kinds of people." He said, "There are two things: one, the recording is going to become part of a court case." He said, "Secondly, I just can't imagine letting families hear this for the first time in a courtroom, or from the media. I feel we should do it."

I had just gotten to the Bureau, and he said, "Why don't you listen to it and tell me what you think." So Sharon and I had a number of conversations. We talked about it, and I think if it hadn't been for Pan Am 103,[5] and my experience in dealing with the families for 11 or 12 years after, I would not have had the same insight. They didn't have a lot of information, and that impacted them for years.

Once I heard the Flight 93 recording, I felt this could answer some questions for people, though it wouldn't answer all the questions. I could see if we played this for them, they would have all of the information that they could possibly have available to them about what happened in the last moment in their loved one's life. This was an extraordinary opportunity for them to have that, and I went back to Acting Director Mueller with

---

[4]   United Airlines Flight 93 was hijacked on 9/11 and crashed into a field near Stonycreek Township, Pennsylvania.

[5]   Pan Am Flight 103 was destroyed by a terrorist bomb on December 21, 1988 over Lockerbie, Scotland.

my recommendation to play it, and he said, "Great. I'll deal with all the fallout." We did it, and we made it available to families. We gave them a choice. We said, "This is what we are going to do. It will be disturbing. You have a choice. You can change your mind right before, or during, or whatever." We did it, and I have to tell you when we look at the different groups of families from 9/11, I think the Flight 93 families have in many ways been able to move forward in ways that a lot of other people haven't.

In the Pentagon, we had a lot of similar kinds of information, although not a voice recorder. I think the families in New York have had the hardest time, because they didn't have the coordinated opportunity to really hear the whole story. Playing the voice recorder of Flight 93 was the right thing to do, and every single one of the people who heard it would say that. We have played it since then for younger family members who were teenagers and children at the time, who wanted to hear it now that they were adults.

Author: It seems like Acting Director Mueller had good intuition, and he didn't let any concerns about what others would say get in the way.

Kathryn Turman: Well, I think that's the sign of really good leaders.

Sharon Bryson: I think that a lot of the people I've worked for, that I considered to be really good leaders, are people who can do just that. They can follow their intuition and their feelings, and they're able to put aside some of the other noises in order to do the right thing. Not everybody has the ability to do that.

****

Sharon's story illustrates how her intuition guided her when the "plan book" didn't cover the extraordinary situation facing her. Sometimes leaders have to go with their gut, just as Acting Director Mueller did. Kathryn's experience with the Pan Am 103 families prepared the way for her recommendation to allow the voice recorder from Flight 93 to be played to family members.

Through these stories of how intuition was used in crisis situations, we can see how important it is to follow your gut, your feelings, your intuition, regardless of what others may think.

****

The stories that follow illustrate how intuition and synchronicity work together in ways that are subtle, yet profound, when we have enough perspective to be able to look back and see how events fit together.

The first story is about John, who spent the time and effort to sit down, do a life review, and share his story. The second story resulted from a conversation that I had with a medical professional.

John's Story

Being a very analytical person (show me the data/facts), I used to think that I didn't listen to my intuition enough. There were times when I had a hunch and regretted not acting accordingly. But now at fifty-something, when I look back at the forks in the road of life so far, I realize that I did hear and heed my intuition when it mattered most.

When I was approaching high school age, my parents encouraged me to apply to a couple of religious institutions, one of which my mother had attended. I think my mother was aware that I had a bit of a rough time at the public middle school (I was always one of the smaller boys), and she was prone to worry. I was accepted at both schools, but nothing inside me was interested. I had heard somehow about a vocational high school in a neighboring town and told my parents that I wanted to learn a trade, because I enjoyed working with my hands. Not sure where that came from, but it's true that as a boy I spent countless hours building models, especially airplanes out of balsa wood. My father was very handy and nurtured my mechanical skills.

At the start of high school, all the freshmen spent a week learning a bit about each trade, then submitted their top-three choices. Mine were electrical, electronics, and machine. Looking back, I think I chose electrical, because I wanted to understand this mysterious, powerful force. I realize now that was probably an early manifestation of a still unconscious quest to become aware of even greater but intangible forces in the universe.

Since I had artistic talent, the Drafting Department Head, and a few other school officials, strongly encouraged me to change my mind. Fortunately, my intuition said, "Stick with your choice." Pencils and T-squares were replaced by computers.

As a sophomore, something motivated me to try out for the soccer team. This seems to have been intuition, since I had never formally played before. I was fortunate to have a great coach, who was patient and encouraging. I didn't have much skill, but I could run, and as he later told me, played with a lot of heart. Through his mentoring and training, I gained much-needed confidence. It was also through soccer that I gained a life-long friend who was key to my career unfolding and two marriages.

As graduation neared, it was time to think about college. Electrical engineering seemed like a logical progression, but I had no idea how much complex math it would require. This is another example of how sometimes it's better to not fully know in advance just what you're getting into. If I had known, I might have shied away and missed the subsequent opportunities.

My high school friend became my college roommate. At the time of college graduation, he interviewed with an aerospace industry recruiter from the west coast and accepted an offer. I still had one more semester to complete a final class. So I stayed behind working at the small company that I had worked at during college, mulling over whether it's better to be a big fish in a small pond, or a small fish in the ocean. I eventually applied to aerospace companies in the northeast and, on a whim, to a government intelligence agency. After returning a long questionnaire, I was invited to DC to take a polygraph test, etc. Then something inside said, "This isn't the right path for you."

I don't know if this is a form of intuition, but around this time of still being young and a bit reckless, there were several occasions when I fell asleep driving home late after dates, etc. Something awakened me just in time to avoid disaster, and I decided to stop pushing my luck and to be more careful.

My old soccer buddy and roommate encouraged me to join him out west. Having someone I knew out west gave me the courage I needed to make the move. I accepted an offer to work where he was employed, and they agreed to a delayed starting date. For some reason, I wanted to wait until the end of summer before moving, Soon after, another engineering student from the same college that I had attended came to work at our company. What started as a summer fling became a serious and intense love affair. We both knew I was leaving and talked about not getting too attached, but we decided that we didn't want to regret not exploring the potential. It hurt so much to say goodbye, but I knew I still had to go without knowing why. The drive out west was a great adventure, but the loneliness hit me hard after being in my new place for a week.

After graduating, she joined me out west, coming to work for a different company. Even though I had doubts she would stick it out if/when things got tough, we married a few years later, and our careers were progressing well. She had an opportunity to advance by moving to the DC area, so I began to look for work there and got an offer soon after. When carrying the last box of personal office stuff out of the building to my car, tears filled my eyes, but my intuition reassured me by sending the message, "You are making the right move at the right time." A year later the marriage was over, but not before a friend of hers introduced us to someone who would become one of my greatest teachers.

One common theme of my career is being thrust into positions of more responsibility without feeling adequately prepared. I've been forced to rely on intuition to navigate around situations where others had strong opinions about what I should or should not do. I've learned it's good to go into some situations without many preconceived notions of the best way to do things. I've grown more attuned to and trusting of my intuition, which has led me to more freedom and peace of mind. But the most rewarding moments have been when intuition guided me in helping to make a positive difference in another's life.

****

John's story points out how intuition and synchronicity may guide us into a relationship that may last a few years and then come to an end. It is not that our intuition was wrong, or the relationship was a failure. The relationship was necessary for one or both of the partners to have an experience that could promote their personal growth and lead them on their life's journey.

****

Susan Kutz's Story

I met Susan Kurtz, a Physician Assistant (PA), when I injured my rotator cuff and made an appointment with her to have my shoulder examined. After an examination, I asked her how she became a PA in orthopedics. She said that she had always been interested in sports, and when her brother broke his arm, she found herself very interested in how bones healed. When it came time for her to pick a career, she started off wanting to be a surgeon, but she did not want to go to school for twelve years. A different path unfolded for her.

Susan graduated from college and was commissioned into the United States Army as a Medical Service Corps Officer. Among her assignments, she had the opportunity to be an administrative assistant in an orthopedic department and really became interested in what they were doing for patients. After moving on from the Army, she obtained her Physician Assistant certification, and then specialized in orthopedics. She is now working in a group practice and loving it. I asked her how intuition played a role in her decisions along the way. She told me that intuition has always played a role, particularly when she decided not to be a surgeon. She laughed when I asked her a question regarding the relationship between her rational mind and her intuition. She said that her intuition led her to the right school, and her mind took all of the courses.

****

Susan's casual observation about the relationship between her mind and her intuition went right to the point: Our intuition suggests that we make a certain decision, and then we decide to follow our intuition and do all of the work.

CHAPTER THREE

GETTING OUT OF OUR WAY

O nce we have decided to follow our intuition, we have to start getting out of our own way. We have to learn what keeps us from following our intuition. Fear is usually what gets in our way. Fear of making a mistake, of what others may think, or of the unknown. What helped me most to follow my intuition was to not over-think a situation in an effort to not make a mistake.

I was relieved to discover that I no longer was expected to know things that I was never designed to know, such as knowing everything, or being in control all of the time. I learned that I couldn't really keep me, or anyone else, safe, or know what was the best thing to do in one situation or another. I believe it comes down to who do we want to trust with our life. Do we want to trust our rational mind to get us through life in the best way possible, or do we want to trust our intuition to guide us? I discovered that I was far better off following my intuition and then showing up to do the work that was in front of me.

Releasing Past Events and Limiting Beliefs

We were born with a fear-based operating system designed to keep us alive and to seek comfort while avoiding discomfort. Our mind operates from a thinking, or rational point of view, while our intuition has no fear and is not constrained by our experiences. We are affected by events in our past, which have created limiting beliefs that constrain us from exercising free will and free choice. Our intuition has no such limits.

If we are going to be able to follow our intuition, we have to discover what prevents us from following intuition's guidance. Our search begins with limiting beliefs that are learned in childhood and are mostly inaccurate, because they are based in fear. We are born knowing that we are unable to protect ourselves and need to rely on others for survival. If we learn that we are safe in the world, we develop differently from a person who learns that life is unsafe. One of our first goals might be to teach ourselves that what we experienced as a child is in the past. Our challenge is to accept the fact that we never got all that we needed and to realize that we cannot resolve the past by looking outside of ourselves. We must accept the reality of the past, and shift from seeking what we need from others to finding everything that we need within ourselves.

Whether we learned that life was safe or not safe, we have probably looked for something outside of ourselves to make us feel better about ourselves, more comfortable. For example, my first car was a 1949 Chevy. It wasn't cool enough, so I bought a 1958 Corvette. Now that was cool. I would pick up my girlfriend at her high school and feel like I was somebody. All the while, of course, I really knew I wasn't anybody, because that is what I was taught as a kid, particularly by my older sister who constantly reminded me of how I was stupid.

The point of my story is to illustrate that we all have been traumatized to some extent. The simplest event can cause trauma, which remains with us, until we discover it and dismantle its associated limiting belief. My belief that I was stupid was dismantled when I completed graduate school. I had to update my limiting belief to match reality.

A way that we can identify a past traumatic event that needs our attention, or change a limiting belief, is to notice how we respond to a situation. We have all had the experience of overreacting to something on television, or to a situation that really gets our dander up. The opposite may also happen, when we find ourselves not reacting when all those around us are. We wonder, "Why don't I react like everyone else?" We must make it our intention to welcome these behavioral clues in order to help us resolve our unconscious conflicts.

In order to become aware of our emotions, we must develop the ability to become our own witness and listen to what's going on moment by moment. First, we must notice when something is off. We can observe that our reaction is out of balance with the situation and wonder, "Why?" This wondering becomes the motivation to change. Change requires a clear intention to unearth our demons, slay our dragons, stand free of our past, and be unafraid of our future.

In order to be unafraid, we must replace our old way of staying safe with a more powerful one. Our old way was based on the myth that we were in control, and that we were smart enough and strong enough to keep ourselves safe. When we discover that we are not equipped to do what we expect, we can surrender our old beliefs and allow a more powerful source to keep us safe—our intuition.

This transition to following our intuition begins by learning to trust that if we follow our intuition, we will be safe and have everything that we need. In fact, we will discover that we have no needs at all. We learn that we have nothing to prove and can allow our intuition to guide us. We want all of our intentions and our endeavors to have a new purpose—to carry out our intuition's guidance.

As we become more secure within ourselves, we can be in very loving relationships without contorting ourselves, because the relationship will not be based on need. Needs are temporary, as are those kinds of relationships. Love-based relationships need nothing beyond the authenticity of the other, because there are no unconscious needs searching for satisfaction.

The process of getting out of our way includes doing the work that shows up for us to do. There will be unfinished business that must be worked through and brought to resolution, so that nothing stands in our way to live free from the unresolved traumas and limiting beliefs from our past. The goal is to continue the practice of following our intuition, as we live through the experiences of our life.

Managing Our Thinking and Focusing Our Awareness

Part of getting out of our way so that we can follow our intuition is to learn to manage our thinking and focus our awareness.

Why do we need to manage our thinking? When our chatterbox thinking is engaged, we have virtually no awareness beyond our own thoughts. This is limiting to our possibilities. Thinking gets in our way and restricts our ability to sense our intuition. As it turns out, we discover that the less chatterbox thinking, the better. Becoming aware requires us to stop thinking too much and to listen and become aware of the moment. Awareness only exists in the moment, so if we are in our heads thinking away, we cannot be aware of anything else. We will only be able to hear our own thoughts.

Just as we manage our chatterbox mind, we want to focus our awareness. Our goal is to be aware of where our awareness is, and where we want it to be. Part of awareness is to have the ability to observe ourselves. We have to see ourselves, before we can change ourselves. We also must take responsibility for our negative or limiting thinking. Most of the time, we will be able to become mindful and aware of what we are thinking. Without the discipline to stop our unconscious ways, we will continue living like we were in the movie, "*Groundhog Day.*"

Another part of awareness, is to develop our ability to constantly listen for guidance from our intuition. Essentially, we want to always be aware of our intuition and any guidance it might have for us. We have to be aware, if we are going to be able to notice what our awareness is noticing. Awareness begins when we are quiet and listening.

Awareness can be focused like a beam of light on a single activity, like when we are passing a large truck at night in heavy rain. We are not thinking about anything except what is going on right in front of us. Continuing with the driving example, when the road is clear and the weather nice and sunny, we can become aware of our surroundings and enjoy the ride. When we are not driving and can sit back and relax, our awareness can expand to the full extent of our senses. As I sit next to the pond in my backyard, I can hear birds, the pond's waterfall, the sound of the mail truck, an airliner passing overhead, and a dog barking in the distance. When we are still, we are able to take in and be aware of all of our senses, including our sixth, which is our intuition.

While our awareness keeps track of the moment, and alert to the traffic, our intuition suggests which way to get to our destination. Imagine what it would look like if we were in our chatterbox mode and unable to hear the directions. We might as well toss a coin to decide which way to go. As an example, I find I do a lot better at driving when I pay attention to my wife, who is reading the map, or giving me directions. She has two rules: rule number one is to always listen to your wife. Rule number two is to always follow rule number one. To be sure, following these rules has insured that I arrive at my destination. Following our intuition will ensure that we fulfill our life's destiny.

Awareness Practices

Here are some practices that you can do to focus your awareness. Start by noticing your thoughts and how your emotions follow along. Emotion always follows a thought, so you can learn the cause of an emotion by searching for its underlying thought. Next, you can notice how what you are thinking influences your mood. At this point, you have a choice whether to keep thinking thoughts that cause you to be uncomfortable, or decide to think more constructive thoughts that will bring you back to the intuitive level of functioning. Awareness will help manage your thinking, so you can enjoy the benefits of being in a relaxed state of mind. This all takes discipline to keep our mind on task. Our mind is not used to being on task. Rather, it is used to wandering all over the place with no particular mission.

When we put our mind to work, we are taking charge and stopping the inner chatter. With awareness as a tool, we are taking charge and giving our mind an expanded mission. We all know that being in the moment is important, but it is hard to stay in the moment. We will get bored and want to get going into the future with our fantasies, or into the past with our assumptions about what has happened. We must recognize this process and prevent it by stopping our automatic thinking and forcing ourselves to provide a new job for our rational mind–the job of becoming more aware.

Trusting Intuition

This new job for our mind of becoming more aware requires us to trust our intuition and listen to its messages in order to become more aware. In fact, asking what our intuition wants us to do will help get us used to trusting it, and keep us at our highest level of functioning. The plan is for us to follow our intuition as much as possible. We will thank ourselves, because we will no longer be expected to know things that we were never designed to know, like knowing what decisions to make that will dictate our future.

As we continue to free ourselves from past conditioning, we become more confident that our future will be taken care of, and that we will fulfill our destiny. We will have no serious questions and can be comfortably in the moment, as we experience our life's journey. It is as if we develop a partnership with our intuition that will navigate us through the opportunities provided by synchronicity, which will get our attention in some way. That's why it is important to notice what we notice.

We notice things for a reason, so it is critical to learn to pay attention and practice following through on what we notice. I noticed a public service announcement asking for volunteers at our local hospice, and the direction of my life changed. Being aware of awareness is like noticing what we notice. Once we notice something, like a public service announcement, we then have the opportunity to make a decision that might change our life. We cannot know at the time of our decision whether we are doing the right thing, or what impact our decision will have on our life. The faster we learn that there are things we will never know or understand, the easier it will be to trust that intuition will never steer us off course.

Learning how to surrender our need to know, and to ask our intuition, is part of getting out of our own way. In fact, most of the time thinking is not required, because the answer will be available to us when we stop thinking and ask our intuition for the solution to our problems. We start out attempting to use our logic and rational thinking to come up with an answer. We try to think about what to do, until we give up and ask. Part of the problem is that we are only able to find solutions from what we believe we know. These solutions are limited by our knowledge and experience. Our intuition is not limited by our past and is able to provide solutions and directions that we would not have considered.

In my experience, the faster I run through all the solutions that I can find, and then decide there are possible solutions that I have not thought of and ask intuition, the less time I spend mulling over the problem. In fact, I have learned to go directly to not knowing and just asking. At times, however, we will find ourselves in situations where there just is not enough time to think through a problem, and we are left with following our gut. I can still remember the look on my wife's face as she stopped on her way out of the door on the way to the Pentagon Family Assistance Center the morning of 9/12 when she said, "I don't know what I'm doing." I told her that she would know when she needed to know. When we are thrust into a crisis situation, we shouldn't expect to know what to do. We can only proceed from moment to moment being guided by our intuition.

An example of the magic of not knowing what to do happened recently when I was confronted with a home maintenance problem. I found water on the basement floor. Water was coming out from under the furnace. I thought that it must have been coming from the humidifier, so I shut off the water to the filter. I still had the problem. Then I took the front panels off of the furnace and looked inside. Sure enough, I found a puddle of water under the fan motor and figured the drain line must have been plugged. I stopped working and planned to call the company that put in the furnace. I figured that I knew what was wrong, and I also knew that I wasn't going to be able to do the repairs. I gave up.

After giving up, I was inspired to look at the installation manual. Reading the directions is always a good idea. It was all like a foreign language, so I found myself just staring at all of the hoses, pipes, and mechanisms. I said to myself, "What do I do now?" Then I saw a rusty spot on the bottom of the unit. Then I saw a drop of water fall from one of the hoses. Eureka! I found a broken hose clamp that was allowing water to leak from the drain system. I replaced a simple clamp.

Synchronicity provided an experience that reinforced the message that not knowing and allowing my intuition to guide me produced good results. When I stopped thinking and got out of my own way, I saw what I needed to see.

CHAPTER FOUR
WAKEUP CALL TO DESTINY

I discovered that I'm not here to pass a test or to be a "good boy." I am really here to participate in a lifetime of experiences that constitute my journey and help me fulfill the purpose of my life. I just can't know what that purpose is. Since I can't know, I might as well follow my bliss and trust that nothing will be left undone. That doesn't mean I can sit back and wait for food to be brought to me. If I did, I would have starved to death a long time ago. Life is hard for a reason. Adversity strengthens our metal, builds our tolerance, and prepares us to take on greater challenges. No experience is wasted, as each provides us something. We will only know what the "something" is in retrospect, when we stop and ask what our experiences are all about.

I was interviewing a client who had gone through the horrible experience of being raped. She asked me why God would allow that to happen. "I don't know," I said. "Why don't you ask and see what comes to mind." She quieted herself and seemed to go inside to another state of mind. Within thirty seconds her eyes snapped open, and she said, "How else could I discover how strong I am." Her comment totally surprised me. In that moment, she was able to put the traumatic experience into a larger perspective and move on with her life, with the rape no longer defining her.

On a less traumatic note, I was flying my trusty airplane one day when the right engine failed. I was hundreds of miles from the nearest land and decided to ask the captain of my aircraft carrier if I could land aboard the ship. I had to let the ship know that I had a single engine and wanted to land as soon as I got back to the ship. This meant that the ship would have to stop getting ready for the next launch and get the deck ready for my arrival. The ship's captain granted permission, and I proceeded to make a perfect landing. Without the failure of the engine, I would have never had the opportunity to discover how well I could make a single-engine landing aboard ship. What started out as a bad situation turned out to be a good one. Of course, at the time, I couldn't know how things were going to turn out. That is where trust comes in. Now I understand that I wouldn't have had the idea to land aboard ship, if I wasn't supposed to have the experience that I needed. This experience happened to be a positive one. If I had crashed on deck, that would have been another kind of experience.

Another experience that I needed happened in the middle of launching an aircraft from the number three catapult. At this time of my life, I was not on any kind of journey that I knew of. I was a pragmatic carrier pilot who was currently one of the catapult officers on the USS Independence (CVA-62). What happened then will stay with me for the rest of my life.

I was about to launch a F-4 Phantom, when I stopped just before giving the signal that would send the fighter from zero to well over a hundred knots in just 178 feet. The aircraft was in afterburner, the pilot had saluted (telling me he was ready to be launched), and I had a clear deck to go ahead and give the launch signal. Something came over me. I froze within inches of completing the launch signal. I stayed frozen in place, not knowing why I froze. Then I saw an aircraft being taxied up the flight deck alongside of the Phantom on the catapult. Still frozen, I watched as the flight deck director turned the taxiing aircraft, so that its tail was right in front of the fighter on the catapult. The pilot's eyes went wide open, as he expected to die in the next moment. I suspended the launch, and we all just looked at each other.

If I had given the launch signal the fighter would have collided with the tail of the taxiing aircraft, causing a massive explosion. The fact that an aircraft was being taxied up the flightdeck alongside the catapult is not out of the ordinary. The problem occurred when the director turned the plane in such a way as to cause its tail to cross in front of the fighter that was about to be launched. This accident was about to happen, and I seemed to know it was coming. The pilot came to me the next day and thanked me for saving his life. I think I said, jokingly, "I was saving mine, and you're welcome."

This experience taught me to always follow my intuition. I believe that was an example of my intuition pushing through and stopping me in my tracks. I definitely was getting information from a source other than my mind. In fact, the event was life-changing. This event, along with several others, began to cause my old normal to come unglued, and a new normal to be formed. By the end of the cruise, I had learned that something bigger than my ego was keeping me alive.

The event that woke me up and put my aviator ego in its place happened on the last day of the cruise. The air wing had flown off the ship the day before, leaving a single F-4 to be launched the next morning. I was standing on four empty acres of flightdeck with only one aircraft to launch. The deck was wet with dew as the F-4 taxied towards the catapult. It had no weapons and minimum fuel, which made it much lighter than normal. Usually an F-4 needs its afterburners to take off, but not this morning.

The pilot went to full power and saluted. He was ready to be launched. I gave the launch signal, and the F-4 started down the catapult track, rotated, and flew off. As he rotated, up came an 8x10 inch steel plate that was hit by the jet blast and started down the deck right at me. I watched it slip and slide on the wet deck, slowly coming towards me. It traveled 180 feet and stopped right between my feet. I bent over, picked it up, and handed it to my catapult captain. Then I looked up and gave thanks that the F-4 was not in afterburner, because if it was, I'd probably have been killed by the steel plate striking me at great speed.

This event "woke me up." I went from being an agnostic to believing in a presence that was guiding my life. I believe this was the moment when I began to believe that there was a larger plan and a journey to be taken. I woke up and recognized that there was a lot more to life than I could imagine. I felt that I was being kept alive to fulfill a purpose. There were just too many times that I could have "bought the farm." Somehow I knew that I wasn't alone. Up until this point in my life, I assumed I was alone, and life was up to me to figure out and find success. My experiences during this cruise as a catapult officer taught me that I was a player on a universal team, and life was a journey.

We are all on a journey, and that by itself is quite a mind expander. In fact, expanding our mind is part of our journey. We must allow our mind to be flexible and hold what we think that we know very loosely. After all, our knowledge is just a placeholder, until new knowledge replaces it.

CHAPTER FIVE
INTUITION IS OUR GUIDE

Intuition wants us to be aware, so that it can guide us through our life. The change that we want to make is to get our mind and intuition working together with our mind releasing control and our intuition taking the lead. When this happens, our intuition becomes our primary source of guidance and always guides us to the best result. When our mind is clear enough to be quiet and create the space for expanded awareness, we will have a clear channel to our intuition. It's as if our mind and intuition work together with no internal conflict.

Our job is to move from surviving life, where we live in accordance with a set of rules and old patterns, to living life in accordance with our true destiny. This doesn't mean that we will avoid all the painful experiences that will come in life. It only means that we will continue to be given what we need to experience in order to fulfill our purpose. We will now be aware of the process and more efficient along our journey.

Looking back over some of my experiences, I can see hints that were directing me to discover the transition from following my mind's directions to following my intuition's guidance. My intuition was hard at work, and at times, had to push into my awareness to get my attention. After more than a few of these experiences, I began to pay attention and listen for intuition's whisper.

Developing Our Inner Witness

One of the tools that helps us listen to our intuition is to monitor our thinking, and continually check on what our intuition has to say. We also can take note of where our mind spends most of its time. Once we notice where our mind is (past, present, or future), we can begin to spend more time in the present, because we know that the past is behind us, and cannot be changed. We also know that we can only fantasize about the future. When I ask my intuition a question about the future, I always get an answer something like, "You will deal with whatever happens, so worrying about the future is a waste of time."

Paying attention to our thinking will make us the witness to our mental process and allow us to take charge of our thoughts. We can observe how our mind is jumping to conclusions, or reacting to a situation. Our job is to bring our mind back to the present moment and just watch what is going on within us and outside of us. This practice of being our own witness will bring us closer to the source of our intuition. The closer we are, the easier it will be to follow its directions, with our mind in the role of doing what intuition suggests.

Intuition is always with us. We just have to teach our mind to pay attention and follow intuition's guidance. My history has taught me that my first impression is usually right. I suggest that you go back and review the times that you didn't follow your initial feeling or thought, and check out what you wish you had done.

I can't count the number of times a client regretted overruling their intuition. They marry someone whom they believe they can fix with enough love. I would hear statements like, "If only I would do or say the right thing, then everything would be alright." Often people stay in abusive relationships, because of the hope that someday the other person will change The fear of change or of being alone keeps people in abusive or loveless situations.

If we believe we need something that we cannot provide within ourselves, then we will seek what we need from outside of ourselves. Having unresolved needs will reduce our ability to exercise our free will and free choice. We will be psychologically limited by our own negative beliefs, and we may be unable to follow our intuition when its guidance differs from what our mind thinks it needs. This is why it is so important for us to pay attention to how we react. If our intuition is guiding us to do something that we can't do, then we know there is work for us to do in order to resolve what is in our way. We want to have a mind that is not being overly influenced, one way or the other.

Tapping into Intuition

Many people ask what they can to do tap into their intuition. Here is a list of five ways that I have found work for me:

1. <u>Recognize when your mind disregards intuition.</u> This takes lots of practice, because the process of disregarding intuition happens so fast. What I have noticed about me might help you find out how your mind disregards your intuitive guidance. Sometimes intuition comes to me as a non-verbal feeling. It is like getting a message that I now have to process and decide what, if anything, to do. I started out ignoring these messages as simply an annoying occurrence. I would shut off the link to my intuition by simply getting into my head and thinking too much. I would find myself making all kinds of excuses about why I did not have to follow my intuition to call a friend. My mind would disregard this suggestion from my intuition and start coming up with all of the reasons not to call. I would think that my call would interrupt what he was doing, or that he would not be home, or any number of other reasons not to call. Fear of being a bother was keeping my mind from following intuition's guidance. Once I realized that I had been conditioned as a child not to bother others, I was able to push past this old belief that I was a bother. I no longer had to disregard my intuitive impulse to contact someone.

While fear might be at the root of not following your intuition, it may be that your mind, like mine, does not like to be interrupted. I will be unconsciously going through my day when an idea enters my mind. I automatically label the idea as distracting and keep moving, ignoring my intuition's attempt to get my attention. It is like my mind is in charge and does not like interruptions. Interruptions cause me to have to stop what I am doing and redirect my attention to something else. When I'm in this mode of operation, I am really unconscious, and my intuition has little chance of getting through to me. The more fixed and rigid my mind is, the less of a chance there is for me to be available to my intuition.

Imagine that we are walking through the woods, paying attention to the path that is right in front of us. Our only goal is to get to where we are going. All the while, our intuition is attempting to get us to slow down and experience the journey. Instead, we keep our head down and have our mind fixed on the endpoint of our trip. It is like we are running in a horserace with blinders that prevent us from being distracted by life. In this case, our mind does not have to disregard intuition, because our mind is so closed that the light of intuition is kept out. While this might be an extreme example of a closed mind, it brings us to the first step in the transition from existing to living. My first step in opening my mind was to recognize that I had blinders on, and I had to take them off. I decided my life was more then getting to its endpoint with the least distraction. I decided to listen for intuitive guidance and pay attention, as would a student trying to learn. Once my mind became used to listening for intuitive guidance, I became more aware of my surroundings and began to slow down and enjoy the journey through the woods. Instead of fixing on a destination, I began to live the experience of each step that I took through life.

2. **<u>Directly ask your intuition a question.</u>** I talk a lot about not knowing and asking, because it's essential for making the space necessary for us to access our intuition. The very act of asking a question means our mind has stopped thinking. Hopefully, it has gone into the listening mode, thereby making space for an answer. When the answer comes, leave it alone. Force yourself not to disregard it. Just sit with the answer, and let it settle in.

Rhetorical questions will not work, because they are not real questions. They are statements in the form of a question. Your mind knows the answer, so new information will be blocked. In fact, the only kind of question that will work is carried by the energy of really not knowing, and comes from a place of honesty without any underlying agenda. We must be mindful of the source of our energy. Is the energy coming from a humble mind that has surrendered to intuition, or from a mind that is looking for a certain answer? Communication is a form of energy and the response that we get is in response to the energy, not the words.

When we ask our question from a place of humility, or not knowing, yet trusting, we will be guided by our intuition. Questions that promote our growth and keep us on our journey are those that I find are answered immediately—even before we can get the question artic-ulated. Questions are linear and the response usually comes as a chunk of energy that we must then put into linear form in order to add the words. The more we ask, the more we will activate the connections that we have between the universe and our intuition. Eventually, our mind will learn to ask constantly, as a way to always remain connected to something greater than itself.

3. **Practice using intuition in your everyday activi-ties.** Start with food selection. Next time you go to the supermarket, plan to ask your intuition to select what it wants you to buy. Put your mind into the witness mode and see what happens, The more you use your intui-tion, the easier it will be for you to tap into it, and the easier it will be for intuition to tap into you. A good example of being connected to our intuition are those instances when we suddenly need to leave the house for an appointment. After driving through town with all of the stoplights and slow drivers, we arrive at our destina-tion to find the perfect parking spot. The really surprising part is when we walk into the meeting room, look at our watch, and see that we are exactly on time, in spite of the delays while driving.

When we stop and look at this example, which has happened to me many times, we can see a pattern that I believe to be at the core of how life works. Intuition told us to leave our house and get started towards our appointment. Our mind knows how to drive the car and negotiate the traffic. Synchronicity sets us up with all the necessary red lights, slow divers, and then provides us a parking place. The interplay of intuition, mind, and synchronicity is a beautiful thing.

4. **Meditate.** For those who meditate, they discover the benefit of being free from their mind's constant chatter. Meditation, along with guided imagery exercises and hypnosis, all serve to suspend critical thinking. With critical thinking suspended, our mind is in the witness mode, which means it is in the audience and not onstage.

There are many kinds of meditation, so I suggest that people find the kind of meditation that feels most comfortable for them. I meditate while walking on a treadmill. I establish a comfortable walking speed, hold onto the side rails and close my eyes. I start paying attention to my breathing: on the in-breath I imagine a pure white light coming into me and on the out-breath I exhaust any negativity, so eventually both in-breath and out-breath are clear and white. While I observe my breathing, I imagine a column of water flowing up through my body and then falling back over the outside of the column and down over my body. It is like I am a water fountain standing in a pool of pure energy that flows up like a fountain and splashes down over me into the pool of light. The benefit that I notice out of this kind of meditation is that the walking helps me control my weight and activates the gray matter of my brain to enhance mental efficiency.

Taking some time each day to mediate, however you do it, will benefit you.

5. **Create space for intuition to communicate.** One day I began my walking exercise thinking about focusing on my heart area and repeating a mantra, "I am walking with my soul." After ten minutes I decided that what I was doing wasn't working, so I changed to just repeating various phrases and noticing how I felt with each one. As the phrases became shorter and shorter, I decided to just walk in silence. After five minutes of internal quiet, I became aware of my feet walking on the treadmill. Then I became aware of the pressure of my shirt on my shoulders, then the temperature of my back. My awareness was expanding. I was starting to get excited, because something was definitely happening.

What happened next was very unexpected. I tried to ask a question about the future and got, "You'll know when the time comes." I tried to ask a question about my past and got, "The past is behind you." Then I couldn't even get the thought of a question to form in my mind, before I became silent. I couldn't think. My mind went silent, and I became just awareness being aware of the stillness.

While I understand the relationship between intuition, mind, and synchronicity, that doesn't mean my life has automatically changed. If only it was that easy. Understanding by itself is not enough to change old behaviors. Behavior changes happen over time, as our new understanding takes over. In the meantime, we need to practice bringing our mind into silence, so that we can spend more time living "in the zone."

When we are functioning without thought, we are "in the zone." There is no thinking when we are in the zone. My granddaughter taught me a lot about being in the zone. After watching a movie that she made, I asked her why acting seemed to come so easy to her. She told me that she memorizes her lines so well that when she is in a scene, she does not think; she moves through the scene in the persona of the character that she is playing. Then I asked her how she came up with the idea to make, star in, edit, direct, and produce her movie. She said that she was sitting around one day with nothing to do, and the idea just "jumped into her head." The movie was very good, and it amazed all who saw it. She was fifteen at the time and unencumbered by experience. She was also sitting around with nothing occupying her mind, thus giving her intuition space to inspire. I don't recommend boredom as a way to tap into our intuition, but having nothing going on in our mind lowers the noise level, so intuition can push through.

I find that anything that we want to do begins with having a clear intention. Then we must have enough discipline to clear our mind of anything that might restrict our ability to listen for intuitive messages. As we recondition our mind to seek out intuition's guidance, we will be bringing our mind into alignment to serve us in the best way possible.

Intuition and Purpose

"Why am I here?" is a common question, or concern. It comes from sensing that we must have some purpose in our life.

I tell my clients that I don't really know the answer to that question. What I do know is that we are not here by accident. Instead of asking why you are here, you might ask for clear guidance from your intuition to complete your journey and your life's purpose and the courage to take advantage of the opportunities that synchronicity provides. To my mind, that is as good as it is going to get. Life is about living the mystery, showing up, and doing the best that we can do. Each of us is on a journey that is guided by our intuition that will take us to and through every experience that we need to fulfill our life's purpose. Synchronicity will be working all of the time to guide us, so we don't really have to worry about it. Knowing why life is what it is, or was what it was, is beyond our reach to understand, and doesn't matter. Even how we label our journey does not change anything. The guidance that we need will always be with us, and synchronicity will always be creating opportunities, regardless of what we do, or don't do, to help us on our way.

I asked my mind to take a timeout and become the silent witness. I was sitting in the sun smoking my cigar and became aware of the wind, the sounds around me, the warmth of the sun, and the swirl of the smoke coming from my cigar. I became aware of the snow melting, and a small trickle of water passing in front of me. As I sat in silence, I became awareness itself, not thinking, not doing, just being fully conscious in a state of potential without a mission. There was no direction to go, no path to follow, no agenda at all. I was simply awareness being aware. There was no movement in any direction. There was only stillness and awareness. A powerful and expanding experience.

Intuition and Synchronicity

Thought creates movement, but without a direction, thought will just wander around with nowhere to go. The role of intuition is to provide us a direction. Then our mind has purpose and can align its resources to follow intuition's guidance. Now we are on our way with a clear direction, and our mind is doing all it can do. All we need now are a set of coincidences that create the opportunities, or openings, for us to pass through. Enter synchronicity. We cannot do a thing about synchronicity. We cannot create it, or stop it from happening. While we can refuse to follow our intuitive guidance, we cannot prevent synchronicity from creating opportunities for us. We can ignore the increasing discomfort created by synchronicity that wants us to quit an abusive workplace situation or a relationship that has run its course. We can say "no" to synchronicity, but synchronicity will not say "no" to us.

CHAPTER SIX

INTUITION AND DESTINY

⊸━━━⊸

As we practice following our intuition, we notice that we are at our best when we follow our intuition and experience the meaningful coincidences that seem to be already in place, waiting and working for us. The less we think about what to do, or not do, and the more we simply respond to what is in front of us, the easier it is for us to be on our path. The more practice we have at just following the clues provided by synchronicity, and acting from our intuition instead of from our mind, the better off we become. If we carry forward this idea of less thinking is better, we end up responding to the clues that point in the direction of our destiny. We simply go where we are intended to go. In following the path of our destiny, we maximize our potential for growth.

Recently, I was driving to a store to buy something that only this particular store carried. I had no idea how to get to the store, so I put the address into my cell phone's navigation system and followed the turn-by-turn directions. I only had to drive the car and didn't have to think about how to get to where I was going. I felt like a field of consciousness in a body going to the store. A parking place presented itself just when I needed one. I went into this huge store, not having a clue as to where to find what I needed. A store associate seemed to appear right in front of me, knew what I wanted, and took me right to where I needed to go, and even pointed to the item that I wanted to buy. Stopping for a moment, and looking at the sequence of events from beginning to end suggests the possibility that everything was set to fall into place for me. Was it fate at work to ensure that I bought this special health product? I don't think that I will ever know for sure.

A more striking experience of this same phenomena happened one early morning on the flight deck of the aircraft carrier USS Independence. (Warning: Here comes another sea story.) I was in flight deck control putting on my gear and preparing for a pre-dawn launch of an E-2 Hawkeye. It was a routine launch of a single aircraft—something we did every morning before normal flight operations began. Suddenly I turned to Carl Jenson, the Aircraft Handling Officer, and told him that something was going to go wrong on the launch. I didn't know exactly what was going to happen, but there was no doubt in my mind that something was going to go wrong. Carl looked at me and sarcastically said something like, "Bryant, get the hell out of here and go do your job." Everyone in flight deck control was laughing, including me.

I walked out of flight deck control and immediately felt the sound of the Hawkeye's turboprop engines. While my sound attenuators kept out the noise, the vibrations bounced off of my chest, causing my insides to vibrate a little. The aircraft was sitting behind the catapult with its lights out, waiting for the signal to taxi forward into launch position. I did my normal inspection of the flight-deck to make sure that the catapult and associated equipment were in place and secure. I was making doubly sure that everything was where it should be. I was still convinced that something was going to go wrong.

The rotating light on the island superstructure went from red to green, indicating that the ship was into the wind, and I had clearance to launch the E-2. I gave the pilot the signal to go to full power. After the normal pause at full power, the E-2's lights came on, indicating the pilot was ready to be launched. I gave the launch signal. The E-2 squatted a little and started down the flightdeck.

Within moments after the Hawkeye started down the deck, I was standing in a cloud of tire smoke. The acrid smell made me hold my breath, as I ran out of the cloud that was now being blown down the deck. I quickly looked forward to see the Hawkeye rotating and beginning its climb to altitude. Then I noticed the two black strips down the deck that were made by tires that were being dragged down the flightdeck. The pilot had left the parking brake on.

I went back into flight deck control and everyone started to sing the theme song from the T.V. series

"*Twilight Zone.*" Some just looked at me funny and asked the obvious question. All I could say was that I didn't know how I knew.

I guess I was really having a twilight zone experience, because I couldn't explain how I knew something was going to happen, before it happened. Unless, of course, fate had ensured that the pilot was going to make the mistake of not releasing the parking brake, before giving me the signal to launch him. Or maybe fate had me set up the experience in order to pick up on fate's energy. I guess fate was at work that early morning, and I felt the incident coming.

I believe that our destiny is influenced by our decisions. Our mind can be a contributor to accomplishing our destiny, or a hindrance. Deciding which path to take in order to fulfill our destiny is no job for our rational mind. Our mind can only fantasize about the future and is vulnerable to being distracted by many things. In addition, thinking is an internal process which reduces our ability to listen to our intuition and notice the clues that are there for us to notice.

When facing a challenging situation, instead of thinking about which direction to take, focus on what is attracting your attention; what are you noticing. All we have to do is step back and really see what is going on. It seems to me that life is purposeful, and our job is to align our consciousness with our destiny, so that we are constantly being guided to follow the path that destiny has prepared for us. The less we interfere with destiny, the more we will be on the path intended for us. We are all here for a reason, so we might as well get out of the way and go along with the program.

The less our ego needs fulfilling, or our rational mind needs to know, explain, or be in control, the better. All we have to do is to choose wisely, and not worry about being wrong, because there is no wrong. Being wrong is a mental assessment.

CHAPTER SEVEN

FINDING OUR WAY

Wouldn't it be fascinating, if we could jump ahead in time and then look back and see the decision that we made to a particularly difficult situation. Did I take the new job and move to California, or did I decline? Did I go ahead with the wedding, or walk away? Since we can't jump ahead, what we can do is ask our intuition a question that will point us in the direction of our destiny. With practice, we learn to stop thinking and simply go where we are directed. We learn that not all decisions are important and define our path. In fact, our destiny accommodates a wide range of choices that are all part of the larger journey.

While most decisions will not change our life, others will. As an example, when I had fulfilled my six-year obligation to the Navy, I had to choose whether to continue to stay in the Navy and make it a career, or resign and pursue a career in the airlines. I went against what many of my friends were doing, and I stayed in the Navy. It just felt right to continue with a Navy career.

Rationally, I could make a case for either decision. The final factor was a feeling. Once I made the decision, I went ahead and rationalized why I decided the way I did.

In retrospect, I can say that I made the right decision for me and my family. I had a successful career, enjoyed flying, and made enough money to support my family. Once my Navy career was over, it came time to make another life-changing decision. So what did I do? I looked for clues. A clue is something that sets itself apart from everything else and causes us to take notice. It is like when I noticed a public service announcement on the radio asking for hospice volunteers. That was a clue that pointed the way to a new career as a social worker.

The idea that there are clues for us to find is very interesting, because it leads us to the conclusion that one path is better than another. While there are many paths available, one is supported by our destiny and will attract all the synchronicity that we need in order to experience what will help us to evolve to our full potential. It is the path that is prepared for us that provides all the meaningful coincidences that we need to stay on track. It is like being a bloodhound tracking a scent that has been left on the ground and that will lead to the catch. While the hound uses scent, we must develop a sense that separates our destiny's path from all of the others that might distract us. Life is full of distractions. Among all of the distractions, there is a best path that is calling to us. The trick is to "sniff" it out and ignore the distractions.

I asked my intuition why following my destiny is so important. The answer came quickly. "Your path keeps you in the cosmic dynamic of evolution. You will touch the lives of others, as others will touch your life, all in service of providing experiences necessary for evolution. Nature is evolving, and humans are part of nature's scheme."

I have discovered that when I get distracted and go off course, I'm not allowed to go too far off before something happens that brings me back on track. The experiences encountered when on a distracted path are not wasted, because they serve to remind us what it feels like to be off course. In fact, I think we have to experience many distractions, before they no longer have any influence over us. Nothing is wasted. Be that as it may, eventually we end up looking for the clues and the synchronicity that signals that we are once again back on our special journey.

Experiencing synchronicity in our life is an indicator that we are on course. Meaningful coincidences are like signposts giving us encouragement to keep going. When everything falls into place and life simply unfolds for us, we know that we are on the right track. When we experience increased discomfort and things do not fall into place, it is time to reassess what we are doing and make some changes. This is what happens when we have been in one place too long and have fallen behind destiny's schedule for us. When we are off course, it feels like having to cut through a jungle with a machete, instead of walking down a trail that was cleared for us ahead of time.

With enough life experience, we are able to look back and see the trail of our decisions. We can see the trail that brought us to where we are in the moment. We can see the consequences of our decisions that were caused by being distracted. I remember feeling really good when I fixed up an old car and sold it, making a profit. I thought that I was pretty smart, so I bought another old car with the plan to fix it up and make more money. The cost to fix the car was much more than it was ever going to be worth. I lost all of my money, when I had to sell it for junk. Fixing up cars for money was a distraction and not part of my destiny. As I look back on how I made the decision to buy another car, I didn't listen to my instincts, and synchronicity was working against me. I was in my head thinking that I knew what I was doing. I did not crosscheck my plan with my intuition. I have learned not to act impulsively without checking with my intuition.

All this is to illustrate how we all will get off course. When this happens, we learn what it feels like and learn more discernment in choosing our direction in life. This is not to say that making good decisions that keep us on course will bring us an easy life. To the contrary, personal growth is painful. Personal growth requires us to stretch our muscles and survive emotional upheaval. We are like a forest that has to go through the destruction of fire in order to burn off the dead-fall and germinate new trees. If we try to tiptoe through life avoiding discomfort, we will be wasting a lifetime. If we spend a lot of time judging everything, we will also be wasting our opportunity to experience life. I have found that keeping my mind open and noticing when my attention has been drawn to something is the best way to find my way

Instead of over thinking and being stuck in our mind, we must be open-minded and aware of the environment around us. This is where we want to be in order to find our way. An open mind is a listening mind. When I received the idea about being a hospice volunteer, I just sat with it. Noticing the announcement in the first place was the universe using synchronicity to point me in the direction that I had to follow in order to experience part of my destiny. I believe the best way for us to find our way is to listen and notice what we notice. Then we must have the courage to take action.

Summary

Life has a purpose. You are not here on earth by accident. You are a contributor to a larger scheme that is beyond your understanding. All you are asked to do is to live out your life the best way possible.

The map that is drawn for you has some trail markers that will help you stay on your pathway through life. These important trail markers are intuition, awareness, and synchronicity.

Think of yourself as an explorer who has been given a map that provides you with all of the information that you will need to embark on a journey of a lifetime. All you will need to get started is the courage to follow your own intuition. Once you commit to the journey, synchronicity will provide the opportunities that you will need to follow your destiny.

ACKNOWLEDGEMENTS

First and foremost, I would like to thank my wife, Meg Falk, for supporting me throughout my journey and for contributing her own story to this project. I want to thank my granddaughter, Angeline Bryant, whose story about making a movie inspired me to look further into the phenomena of intuition and synchronicity. The contributions of Kathryn Turman, Sharon Bryson, Susan Kutz, and John provided the centerpiece of the project and brought the book to life. I want to thank my friends, Tom Murphy and Ilona Kastenhofer, who took time out of their schedules to read and comment on the book.

I thank my extraordinary editor, Sharon K. Hall, who has contributed in so many ways to my being able to share my experiences and those of my wonderful contributors. To the many others who have listen to my account of writing this book, I am forever grateful.